SRA Open Court Reading

Level 1 • Book 1

Keep Trying

•

Games

OPEN COURT READING

Level 1 • Book 1

— PROGRAM AUTHORS —

Marilyn Jager Adams	Jan Hirshberg	Marsha Roit
Carl Bereiter	Anne McKeough	Marlene Scardamalia
Joe Campione	Michael Pressley	Gerald H. Treadway, Jr.

SRA

A Division of The McGraw·Hill Companies

Columbus, Ohio

Acknowledgments

Grateful acknowledgment is given to the following publishers and copyright owners for permissions granted to reprint selections from their publications. All possible care has been taken to trace ownership and secure permission for each selection included. In case of any errors or omissions, the Publisher will be pleased to make suitable acknowledgments in future editions.

Keep Trying

From THE ITSY BITSY SPIDER, Text and illustration copyright © 1993 by Iza Trapani. All rights reserved. Used with permission by Charlesbridge Publishing, Inc.

"The Kite" from DAYS WITH FROG AND TOAD by Arnold Lobel. COPYRIGHT © 1979 BY ARNOLD LOBEL. Used by permission of HarperCollins Publishers.
"The Garden" from FROG AND TOAD TOGETHER by Arnold Lobel. COPYRIGHT © 1971, 1972 BY ARNOLD LOBEL. Used by permission of HarperCollins Publishers.
From Kazue Mizumura's The Way of an Ant, copyright © 1970 by Kazue Mizumura, Thomas Y. Crowell Company. Reprinted with permission of copyright holder.

"The Hare and the Tortoise" from THE BEST OF AESOP'S FABLES Text © Copyright 1990 by Margaret Clark; Illustrations © 1990 by Charlotte Voake. Reproduced by permission of Candlewick Press Inc., Cambridge, MA, on behalf of Walker Books Ltd., London.

"74th Street" from THE MALIBU AND OTHER POEMS by Myra Cohn Livingston. Copyright © 1972 by Myra Cohn Livingston. Reprinted by permission of Marian Reiner.

Games

"A Game Called Piggle" from PIGGLE by Crosby Bonsall. Copyright © 1973 by Crosby Bonsall. Used by permission of HarperCollins Publishers.

JAFTA by Hugh Lewin illustrations by Lisa Kopper. Copyright 1983 by Hugh Lewin. Published by Carolrhoda Books, Inc. A division of Lerner Publishing Group. All rights reserved.

From MATTHEW AND TILLY by Rebecca C. Jones, copyright © 1991 by Rebecca C. Jones, text. Used by permission of Dutton Children's Books, an imprint of Penguin Putnam Books for Young Readers, a division of Penguin Putnam Inc. From MATTHEW AND TILLY by Rebecca C. Jones, illustrated by Beth Peck, copyright © 1991 by Beth Peck, illustrations. Used by permission of Dutton Children's Books, an imprint of Penguin Putnam Books for Young Readers, a division of Penguin Putnam Inc.

From THE GREAT BALL GAME: A MUSKOGEE STORY by Joseph Bruchac, copyright © 1994. Pictures Copyright © by Susan L. Roth, 1994. Reproduced by arrangement with Dial Books for Young Readers, a division of Penguin Putnam Inc.

"The Big Team Relay Race" from ON YOUR MARK, GET SET, GO! BY LEONARD KESSLER. COPYRIGHT © 1972 BY LEONARD KESSLER. Used by permission of HarperCollins Publishers.

Photo Credits

24 courtesy of Iza Trapani; 82 © Laurel Aiello; 84 Gift of Stephen C. Clark, B.A., 1903, Yale University Art Gallery. © 2001 Estate of Pablo Picasso/Artist Rights Society (ARS), New York. Photo: Francis G. Mayer/Corbis; 85 (t) Jointly owned by the Norton Simon Art Foundation, Pasadena, California and The J. Paul Getty Museum, Malibu, California, (b) The Seattle Art Museum, Purchased with funds from P.O.N.C.H.O.; 90 (t) © Archive Photos; 96 (b) © Walker Books Limited; 122 © Mark Lawrence; 130 (t) Acquisition in memory of Mitchell A. Wilder, Director, Amon Carter Museum, 1961-1979. Amon Carter Museum, Fort Worth, Texas. 1979.4, (b) The Seattle Art Museum, Gift of Katherine White and the Boeing Company; 131 (t) Gift of the Harmon Foundation, National Museum of American Art, Smithsonian Institution, Washington, DC. Photo: Art Resource, NY, (b) © Scala/Art Resource, NY; 152 (t) © Dutton, (b) © Beth Peck; 194 (b) © Charmie Curran.

Unit Opener Illustrations

10–11 Brian Karas; 100–101 Hilary Knight.

www.sra4kids.com

SRA/McGraw-Hill

A Division of The McGraw-Hill Companies

Program Authors

Marilyn Jager Adams, Ph.D.
BBN Technologies

Carl Bereiter, Ph.D.
University of Toronto

Joe Campione, Ph.D.
University of California at Berkeley

Jan Hirshberg, Ed.D.
Reading Specialist

Anne McKeough, Ph.D.
University of Calgary

Michael Pressley, Ph.D.
University of Notre Dame

Marsha Roit, Ph.D.
National Reading Consultant

Marlene Scardamalia, Ph.D.
University of Toronto

Gerald H. Treadway, Jr., Ed.D.
San Diego State University

Table of Contents

Table of Contents

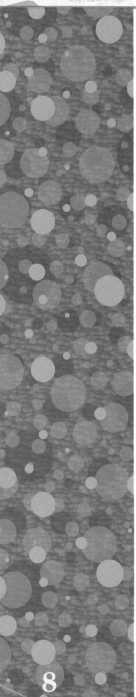

Keep Trying

Have you ever tried very, very hard to learn something new or maybe to build something? Was it hard to learn to ride a bike or to in-line skate? Did you keep trying until you finally learned? How did it feel?

The Itsy Bitsy Spider

as told and illustrated by Iza Trapani

The itsy bitsy spider
Climbed up the waterspout.
Down came the rain
And washed the spider out.

Out came the sun
And dried up all the rain,
And the itsy bitsy spider
Climbed up the spout again.

The itsy bitsy spider
Climbed up the kitchen wall.
Swoosh! went the fan
And made the spider fall.

Off went the fan.
No longer did it blow.
So the itsy bitsy spider
Back up the wall did go.

The itsy bitsy spider
Climbed up the yellow pail.
In came a mouse
And flicked her with his tail.

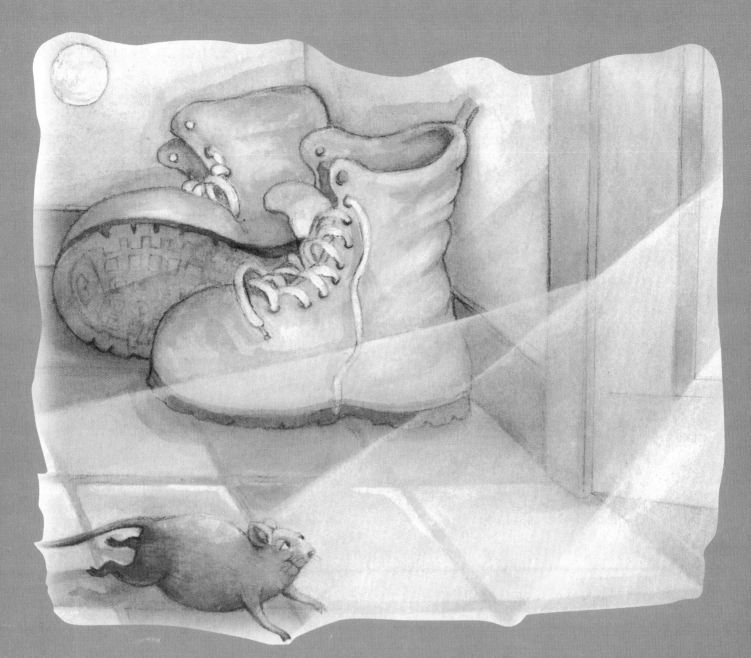

Down fell the spider.
The mouse ran out the door.
Then the itsy bitsy spider
Climbed up the pail once more.

The itsy bitsy spider
Climbed up the rocking chair.
Up jumped a cat
And knocked her in the air.

Down plopped the cat
And when he was asleep,
The itsy bitsy spider
Back up the chair did creep.

The itsy bitsy spider
Climbed up the maple tree.
She slipped on some dew
And landed next to me.

20

Out came the sun
And when the tree was dry,
The itsy bitsy spider
Gave it one more try.

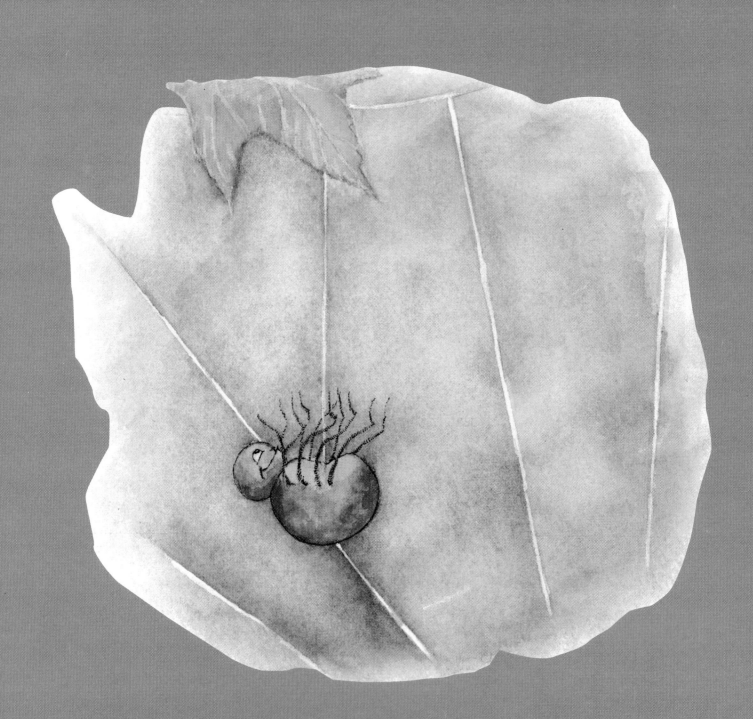

The itsy bitsy spider
Climbed up without a stop.
She spun a silky web
Right at the very top.

She wove and she spun
And when her web was done,
The itsy bitsy spider
Rested in the sun.

The Itsy Bitsy Spider

Meet the Author and Illustrator

Iza Trapani was born in Poland. Now she lives in New York. She has written and illustrated many children's books. Many of the books Iza Trapani has illustrated include animals because she likes them so much. She also enjoys being in the mountains, where she likes to climb, bike, and ski.

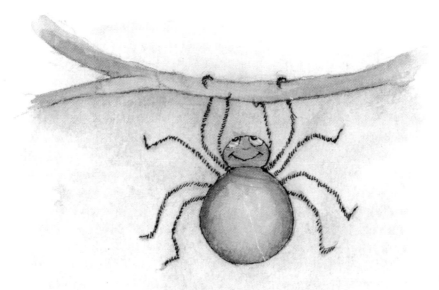

Theme Connections

Within the Selection

Read the questions below, and think about your answers. In small groups, discuss your ideas with one another. Then choose a person to report your group's answers to the class.

- What was the itsy bitsy spider really trying to do?
- When things got in her way, what did the spider do?

Beyond the Selection

- Think about the itsy bitsy spider. What does she teach you about trying?
- Add items to the Concept/Question Board about trying.

Toad heard laughter.
Three robins were sitting in a bush.
"That kite will not fly," said the robins.
"You may as well give up."

Toad ran back to Frog.
"Frog," said Toad,
"this kite will not fly.
I give up."

"We must make a second try,"
said Frog. "Wave the kite
over your head. Perhaps
that will make it fly."

Toad ran back
across the meadow.
He waved the kite
over his head. The kite went up
in the air and then fell down
with a thud.

"What a joke!" said the robins.
"That kite will never
get off the ground."

"We ow again.
a thirdead.
"Wave
and ju nd
Perhap.

"That kite is junk,"
said the robins. "Throw it
away and go home."

Toad ran back to Frog.
"This kite is junk," he said.
"I think we should throw it
away and go home."

"Toad," said Frog,
"we need one more try.
Wave the kite over your head.
Jump up and down
and shout UP KITE UP."
Toad ran across the meadow.
He waved the kite over his head.
He jumped up and down.
He shouted, "UP KITE UP!"

The kite flew into the air.
It climbed higher and higher.

"We did it!" cried Toad.
"Yes," said Frog.
"If a running try
did not work,
and a running and waving try
did not work,
and a running, waving,
and jumping try
did not work,

I knew that
a running, waving, jumping,
and shouting try
just had to work."

The robins flew out of the bush.
But they could not fly as high
as the kite.

Frog and Toad sat and watched their
kite. It seemed to be flying way up at
the top of the sky.

The Kite

Meet the Author and Illustrator

Arnold Lobel began his career as an illustrator. Then he started to write his own stories. Most of them were about animals, including frogs, toads, grasshoppers, and mice.

Theme Connections

Within the Selection

Read the questions below, and think about your answers. In small groups, discuss your ideas with one another. Then choose a person to report your group's answers to the class.

- Why did Toad keep wanting to give up?
- Why did Frog want to keep trying?

Across Selections

- What do Frog and the itsy bitsy spider teach you about trying?

Beyond the Selection

- Think about how "The Kite" adds to what you know about reaching a goal.
- Add items to the Concept/Question Board about trying.

Focus Questions If you try to grow a garden, what do seeds need to grow? How long does it take for a seed to grow?

The Garden

Arnold Lobel

Frog was in his garden. Toad came walking by. "What a fine garden you have, Frog," he said.

"Yes," said Frog. "It is very nice, but it was hard work."

"I wish I had a garden," said Toad.

"Here are some flower seeds. Plant them in the ground," said Frog, "and soon you will have a garden."

"How soon?" asked Toad.

"Quite soon," said Frog.

Toad ran home. He planted the flower seeds. "Now seeds," said Toad, "start growing."

Toad walked up and down a few times.
The seeds did not start to grow. Toad put
his head close to the ground and said
loudly, "Now seeds, start growing!"

Toad looked at the ground again. The seeds did not start to grow. Toad put his head very close to the ground and shouted, "NOW SEEDS, START GROWING!"

Frog came running up the path. "What is all this noise?" he asked.

"My seeds will not grow," said Toad.

"You are shouting too much," said Frog. "These poor seeds are afraid to grow."

"My seeds are afraid to grow?" asked Toad.

"Of course," said Frog. "Leave them alone for a few days. Let the sun shine on them, let the rain fall on them. Soon your seeds will start to grow."

That night Toad looked out of his window. "Drat!" said Toad. "My seeds have not started to grow. They must be afraid of the dark."

Toad went out to his garden with some candles. "I will read the seeds a story," said Toad. "Then they will not be afraid."

Toad read a long story to his seeds.

All the next day Toad sang songs to his seeds.

And all the next day Toad read poems
to his seeds.

And all the next day Toad played
music for his seeds.

Toad looked at the ground. The seeds still did not start to grow.

"What shall I do?" cried Toad. "These must be the most frightened seeds in the whole world!"

Then Toad felt very tired, and he fell asleep.

"Toad, Toad, wake up," said Frog.
"Look at your garden!"

Toad looked at his garden. Little green plants were coming up out of the ground.

"At last," shouted Toad, "my seeds
have stopped being afraid to grow!"

"And now you will have a nice garden
too," said Frog.

"Yes," said Toad, "but you were right,
Frog. It was very hard work."

The Garden

Meet the Author and Illustrator

Arnold Lobel was a daydreamer. When he was a child, he wrote stories and drew pictures for his classmates. He loved to hear Mother Goose stories. When he grew up, Arnold illustrated his favorite Mother Goose rhymes.

Theme Connections

Within the Selection

Read the questions below, and think about your answers. In small groups, discuss your ideas with one another. Then choose a person to report your group's answers to the class.

- How did Toad keep trying to make his seeds grow?
- Did Toad need to try so hard to make his seeds grow?

Across Selections

- How was the way Toad kept trying in "The Garden" different from the way the itsy bitsy spider kept trying?

Beyond the Selection

- Think about what "The Garden" teaches you about trying to reach a goal.
- Add items to the Concept/Question Board about trying.

Focus Questions Have you learned something, and then decided to learn something more difficult? Have you helped someone younger than you learn something new?

The Way of an Ant

Kazue Mizumura

illustrated by Laurel Aiello

Once there was a young ant who wanted to climb as high as the blue sky. He started to climb the tallest blade of grass he could find.

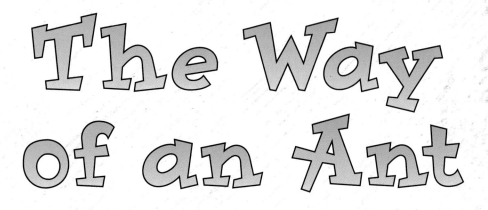

When he reached the tip of the grass,
he looked up, and saw that a dandelion
stood even higher.
He raced down to the ground and started
to climb up the dandelion.

When he reached the top of the dandelion,
he looked up, and there against the sky
he saw a rose,
stretching its stem as high as it could go.
He hurried down to the ground and started
to climb up the stem of the rose.

When he reached the rose,
he stopped awhile to smell its petals.
Then he thought he saw the sun in the sky.
But it was only a sunflower's
golden ring, shining
high above the rose.
He tumbled down to the ground and started
to climb up the sunflower.

When he reached the face of the sunflower,
a gnarled branch of an apple tree
with three green apples
hung over him.
He quickly ran down to the ground and started
to climb up the apple tree.

When he reached the top of the apple tree,
he looked up and saw a maple tree
shading him from the sky with
its fanlike leaves.
He rushed down to the ground and started
to climb up the maple tree.

When he reached the top of the maple
tree, he took a deep breath
and looked around for the sky.
But there was an enormous oak tree
towering over the whole field.
He ran down to the ground,
dashed across the field, and started
to climb up the oak tree.

When he reached the top of the oak tree,
he was very tired.
But the higher he climbed,
the higher he wanted to climb.

Then he saw a pine tree
on a faraway hilltop
reaching up to the sky.
He went down again to the ground,
ran to the hilltop, and started
to climb the pine tree.

When he reached the top of the pine tree,
there was the blue sky as far as he could see.
And there were mountains beyond mountains
and trees beyond trees,
enough for him to climb forever.

And there he saw
the pine tree
the oak tree
the maple tree
the apple tree
the sunflower
the rose
the dandelion
and the grass.

How surprised he was to see
how hard he had tried.
How happy he was to have
climbed so high.

But now he was much older
and a little wiser, and
he would climb no more.

He started down,
and on the way he met a young ant
rushing and puffing to climb up to
the sky.
The old ant smiled and nodded
at the young ant, and passed
without saying a word.

The Way of an Ant

Meet the Author

Kazue Mizumura began her career as an illustrator. Her interest in art began as a child living in Japan. "I always liked to draw and that was the only thing I could do really well . . . [in] school." After she moved to the United States, she was encouraged to write her own stories. Now she writes and illustrates her own books.

Meet the Illustrator

Laurel Aiello has illustrated for textbooks, party books, cookbooks, and storybooks. She says of this particular story, "Since I have always liked to draw animals, I found it especially fun to illustrate this story about an adventurous ant. I tried to make him 'come alive' for you as he travels through the world of grass, flowers, and trees."

Theme Connections

Within the Selection

Read the questions below, and think about your answers. In small groups, discuss your ideas with one another. Then choose a person to report your group's answers to the class.

- Why did the ant want to climb as high as the sky?
- Why did the ant decide to stop climbing?

Across Selections

- How is what the ant learned about trying different from what Toad learned in "The Kite"?

Beyond the Selection

- Think about what "The Way of an Ant" says about reaching your goals.
- Add items to the Concept/Question Board about trying.

First Steps. 1943. **Pablo Picasso.** Oil on canvas. Yale University Art Gallery. ©2001 Estate of Pablo Picasso/Artist Rights Society (ARS), New York.

Waiting. c. 1882. **Edgar Degas.** Pastel on paper. 19 × 24 in. Jointly owned by the Norton Simon Art Foundation, Pasadena, California and the J. Paul Getty Museum, Malibu, California.

Study for the Munich Olympic Games Poster. 1971. **Jacob Lawrence.** Gouache on paper. The Seattle Art Museum.

Focus Questions Will you always get what you want when you try hard? What if we try something and it doesn't work out?

The Fox and the Grapes

Aesop
illustrated by Judith Moffatt

One day a fox was running down a dusty road. He was hot and thirsty. Soon he saw some grapes hanging on a vine in a garden.

The grapes were large and ripe
and juicy. They looked very tasty
to the hot, thirsty fox.
    "How I wish I had some
of those grapes," said the fox.

The fox jumped high in the air. He reached up with his paw, but he did not get the grapes.

He jumped higher and higher, but he still could not get the grapes.

At last the fox gave up.

"Those grapes can stay on the vine," said the fox. "I can tell that they are sour. They must taste awful. I don't like sour grapes."

The Fox and the Grapes

Meet the Author

Aesop lived nearly 3,000 years ago in Greece. He was known for teaching people by telling funny little stories. Aesop remembered hundreds of these stories, yet he never wrote any of them down. The stories he told are still popular today.

Meet the Illustrator

Judith Moffatt has illustrated more than 23 books, including some she also has written. She knew in high school that she wanted to be an artist, but says her interest in cut paper art began with the beautiful papers her dad brought home from the printing company where he worked. Judith has received many awards for her art.

Theme Connections

Within the Selection

Read the questions below, and think about your answers. In small groups, discuss your ideas with one another. Then choose a person to report your group's answers to the class.

- What did the fox try to do?
- Why did the fox say the grapes were sour?

Across Selections

- What might the ant in "The Way of an Ant" say to the fox about trying?

Beyond the Selection

- Think about a time when someone you know acted like the fox.
- Add items to the Concept/Question Board about trying.

Focus Questions Does the fastest runner always win every race? Can you be successful if you work slowly?

The Hare and the Tortoise

from THE BEST OF AESOP'S FABLES

Aesop

retold by Margaret Clark

illustrated by Charlotte Voake

A hare was one day making fun of a tortoise. "You are a slowpoke," he said. "You couldn't run if you tried."

"Don't laugh at me," said the tortoise. "I bet that I could beat you in a race."

"Couldn't," replied the hare.

"Could," replied the tortoise.

"All right," said the hare. "I'll race you. But I'll win, even with my eyes shut."

They asked a passing fox to set them off.

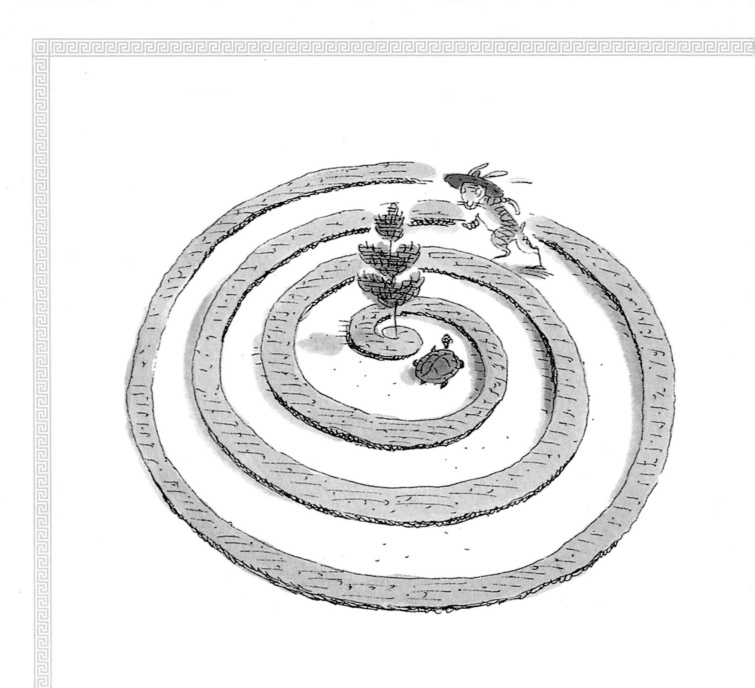

"Ready, set, go!" said the fox.

The hare went off at a great pace. He got
so far ahead he decided he might as well
stop for a rest. Soon he fell fast asleep.

The tortoise came plodding along,
never stopping for a moment.

When the hare woke up, he ran as fast as he could to the finish line.

But he was too late—the tortoise had already won the race!

The Hare and the Tortoise

Meet the Authors

Aesop traveled a lot, telling wise and entertaining fables. A fable is a very short story that teaches a lesson. Aesop told many fables using animal characters.

Margaret Clark began to write stories for her children when they were very little. Her children and her stories grew up together. Clark likes to write about things she has done, like camping, but has also retold stories done by other people, such as Aesop, in a new way.

Meet the Illustrator

Charlotte Voake always wanted to be an illustrator. She won a poster contest when she was twelve. She published her first book while she was still in college. She lives in England and enjoys sailing when she isn't drawing.

Theme Connections

Within the Selection

Read the questions below, and think about your answers. In small groups, discuss your ideas with one another. Then choose a person to report your group's answers to the class.

- Which animal tried the hardest to win the race?
- Why did the other animal lose?

Across Selections

- How is the tortoise like the ant in "The Way of an Ant?

Beyond the Selection

- Think how this story adds to what you already know about trying.
- Add items to the Concept/Question Board about trying.

Focus Questions Have you ever gotten hurt
when you tried something new?
Did you keep trying?

74th Street

Myra Cohn Livingston
illustrated by Stella Ormai

Hey, this little kid gets roller skates.
She puts them on.
She stands up and almost
flops over backwards.
She sticks out a foot like
she's going somewhere and
falls down and

smacks her hand. She
grabs hold of a step to get up and
sticks out the other foot and
slides about six inches and
falls and
skins her knee.

And then, you know what?

She brushes off the dirt and the
blood and puts some
spit on it and then
sticks out the other foot

again.

We all like to play games. But can we learn from games, too? Maybe we can. See what Homer and Bear, Jafta, Matthew and Tilly, and the animals find out about themselves while playing games.

Theme Connections

Within the Selection

Read the questions below, and think about your answers. In small groups, discuss your ideas with one another. Then choose a person to report your group's answers to the class.

- How many people are needed to play "Mary Mack"?
- Which words rhyme in "Mary Mack"?

Across Selections

- What other game have you read about that used rhyming words?

Beyond the Selection

- Think about other things you could do as you recite "Mary Mack."
- Add items to the Concept/Question Board about games.

Ballplay of the Sioux on the St. Peters River in Winter. 1848. **Seth Eastman.** Oil on canvas. Amon Carter Museum, Fort Worth, Texas.

Game Board. Twentieth century. **Dan People**. Liberia. Wood and metal. The Seattle Art Museum.

He jumped so high, high, high,
That he reached the sky, sky, sky,
And he didn't come back, back, back,
'Til the Fourth of July, 'ly, 'ly.

Mary Mack

Meet the Illustrator

Bob Barner studied art in college and became an art teacher. Now he likes to write and illustrate books. "Most of my work [begins] by simple doodles," he says. Now he lives and works in Boston, Massachusetts.

She asked her mother, mother, mother,
For fifty cents, cents, cents,

To watch the elephant, elephant, elephant,
Jump over the fence, fence, fence.

Theme Connections

Within the Selection

Read the questions below, and think about your answers. In small groups, discuss your ideas with one another. Then choose a person to report your group's answers to the class.

- Do you think Jafta was really with the animals in the story?
- How did Jafta have fun?

Across Selections

- How was the game that Jafta played like the game that Bear played?

Beyond the Selection

- Think how Jafta's game is like other games you have played.
- Add items to the Concept/Question Board about games.

Focus Questions Do you know any
hand-clapping games? Do games
always have a winner?

Mary Mack

illustrated by Bob Barner

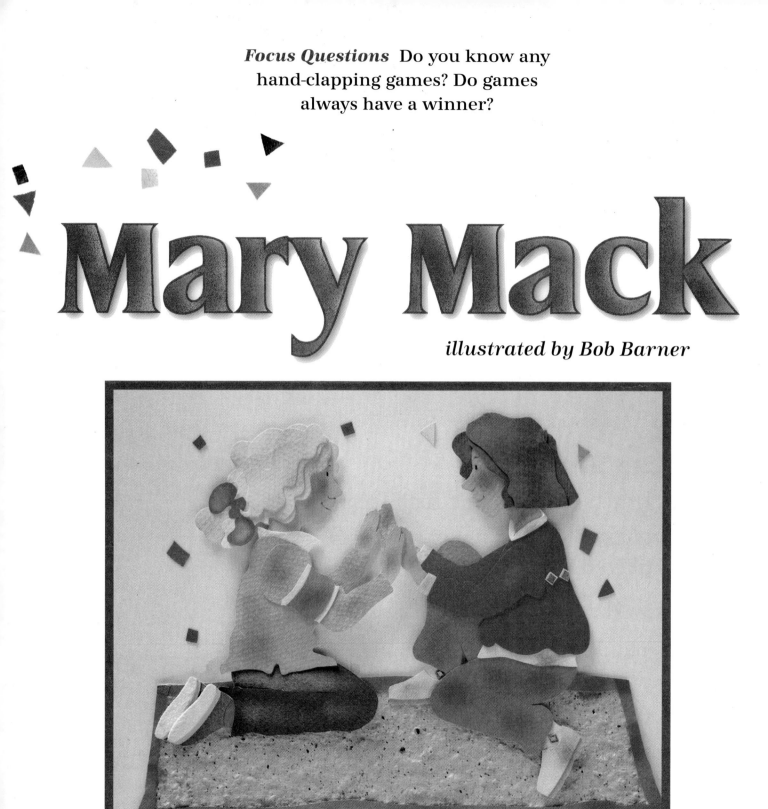

Oh, Mary Mack, Mack, Mack,
All dressed in black, black, black,
With silver buttons, buttons, buttons,
All down her back, back, back.

But actually, said Jafta,
I don't think there's anything quite so
nice as being a flamingo flying off into
the sunset . . .

Jafta

Meet the Author

Hugh Lewin was born in Lydenburg, South Africa; however, his family was from England. Hugh moved to England as an adult. He later wrote the Jafta stories to teach his daughters about where he grew up in South Africa.

Meet the Illustrator

Lisa Kopper grew up in Chicago, Illinois. When she was in her twenties, she moved to England where she became an illustrator. Since then she has illustrated more than 100 children's books, many of which have been published throughout the world. She is well-known for her multicultural work, of which the Jafta Family Series is the most famous.

Sometimes I want to be as tall as a giraffe, as long as a snake.

And I want to run as fast as a cheetah, as quick as an ostrich,

or swing through the trees like a monkey, and fly high high high like an eagle,

or just stand very still, like a crane on one leg.

or just nuzzle like a rabbit.

When I get tired, I like lazing in the
sun like a lizard,
or wallowing warm like a hippo,
and feeling cuddly like a lamb.

But when I get cross, I stamp like an elephant and grumble like a warthog.

(I don't often get cross, said Jafta.)

And I can be as strong as a rhino.

or skip like a spider,

or laugh like a hyena.

And sometimes I want to jump like
an impala,

and dance like a zebra,

SCHOOL

IN

OUT

101

Focus Questions Have you and a friend ever made up your own game? What words rhyme with "piggle"?

A Game Called Piggle

from PIGGLE

Crosby Bonsall

"Oh, Bear," Homer said, "will you play a game with me?"
Bear said, "Yes, I will. What shall we play?"

"Do you know a game called
Piggle?" Homer asked.
"Piggle . . . Piggle," Bear said.
"Piggle like triggle, hmmmm."

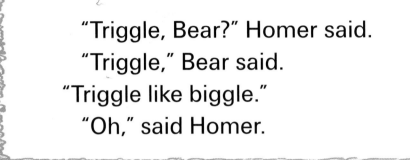

"Triggle, Bear?" Homer said.
"Triggle," Bear said.
"Triggle like biggle."
"Oh," said Homer.

"Let me think," said Bear.
"Piggle like miggle."
"Miggle, Bear?" Homer said.
"Miggle like diggle," Bear said.
"Oh," said Homer.

"Give me time," said Bear.
"Let me see now, we have triggle and biggle, miggle and diggle like Piggle."

"Oh, *I* see," cried Homer. "Let me try.
Wiggle, giggle, sniggle and figgle
like Piggle. That's *it*, Bear. I can play!"

"Yes, you can," cried Bear.
"Maybe I know the game of Piggle
after all. It sounds nice."
"Yes, it does," Homer said.
"Let's piggle some more.
Ishy, wishy, fishy, dishy."

Bear sang, "Diddley, widdley, fiddley, riddley."
And together they sang, "Mumpity, wumpity, dumpity, lumpity."

109

A Game Called Piggle

Meet the Author and Illustrator

Crosby Bonsall was born in Queens, New York. She was always interested in art and went to school to study it. After graduating, she worked for advertising firms. She later wrote and drew illustrations for more than 40 children's books. Sometimes she wrote and illustrated her stories using the last name Newell, her last name before she got married.

Theme Connections

Within the Selection

Read the questions below, and think about your answers. In small groups, discuss your ideas with one another. Then choose a person to report your group's answers to the class.

- What kind of game was Piggle?
- Did Bear know the game of Piggle?

Beyond the Selection

- Think about games like Piggle that you have played.
- Add items to the Concept/Question Board about games.

Focus Questions When you play make-believe games, what do you pretend to be? If you could be an animal, what animal would you be?

Jafta

A Shared Reading Story
Hugh Lewin
illustrated by Lisa Kopper

When I'm happy, said Jafta, I purr like a lioncub,

112

Focus Questions What games do you play with your friends? Why do we sometimes not get along with friends when we play games?

Matthew and Tilly

Rebecca C. Jones
illustrated by Beth Peck

Matthew and Tilly were friends.

They rode bikes together, and they
played hide-and-seek together.

They sold lemonade together.
When business was slow, they
played sidewalk games together.

And sometimes they ate ice-cream
cones together.

Once they even rescued a lady's
kitten from a tree together.

The lady gave them money for the
bubble-gum machines.
So later they chewed gum together
and remembered how brave they
had been.

Sometimes, though, Matthew and
Tilly got sick of each other.

One day when they were coloring,
Matthew broke Tilly's purple crayon.
He didn't mean to, but he did.
  "You broke my crayon," Tilly said in
her crabbiest voice.

"It was an old crayon," Matthew said in his grouchiest voice. "It was ready to break."

"No, it wasn't," Tilly said. "It was a brand-new crayon, and you broke it. You always break everything."

"Stop being so picky," Matthew said.
"You're always so picky and stinky
and mean."
　"Well, you're so stupid," Tilly said.
"You're so stupid and stinky and mean."

Matthew stomped up the stairs. By himself.

Tilly found a piece of chalk and
began drawing numbers and squares
on the sidewalk. By herself.

Upstairs, Matthew got out his cash register and some cans so he could play store. He piled the cans extra high, and he put prices on everything.

This was the best store he had ever made. Probably because that picky and stinky and mean old Tilly wasn't around to mess it up.

But he didn't have a customer. And playing store wasn't much fun without a customer.

Tilly finished drawing the numbers and squares. She drew them really big, with lots of squiggly lines. This was the best sidewalk game she had ever drawn.

Probably because that stupid and stinky and mean old Matthew wasn't around to mess it up.

But she didn't have anyone to play with. And a sidewalk game wasn't much fun without another player.

Matthew looked out the window
and wondered what Tilly was doing.

Tilly looked up at Matthew's window
and wondered what he was doing.

She smiled, just a little. That was
enough for Matthew.
"I'm sorry," he called.
"So am I," said Tilly.

And Matthew ran downstairs so
they could play.
Together again.

Matthew and Tilly

Meet the Author

Rebecca C. Jones used her toys to create adventure stories when she was very young. "I rescued them from kidnappers, pushed them out of the way of speeding trucks, and caught them as they fell from helicopters," she remembers. When she grew older, Rebecca became a reporter to write about real-life stories. She began writing books for kids about real life, like *Matthew and Tilly*, after her own children were born.

Meet the Illustrator

Beth Peck studied drawing at art school and has illustrated many books and stories. Being an illustrator is a dream come true for her. She says it is important to have dreams and to work hard in order to succeed.

Theme Connections

Within the Selection

Read the questions below, and think about your answers. In small groups, discuss your ideas with one another. Then choose a person to report your group's answers to the class.

- Why did Matthew and Tilly stop playing with each other?
- Why did Matthew and Tilly decide to be friends again?

Across Selections

- In what other story is getting along important? Why?

Beyond the Selection

- Think about the kinds of problems that friends can have when they play together.
- Add items to the Concept/ Question Board about games.

The Great Ball Game

A Muskogee Story

adapted from the story retold by Joseph Bruchac
illustrated by Susan L. Roth

Characters

Storyteller	Bird 1
Bear	Bird 2
Crane	Animal 1
Bat	Animal 2
Fox	Birds
Deer	Animals
Hawk	

Storyteller: Long ago the Birds and Animals had a great argument.

Birds: We who have wings are better
than you.

Animals: That is not so. We who have teeth
are better.

Birds:	No. We who have wings are better.
Animals:	No, you are not. We who have teeth are better.
Birds:	No. We who have wings are better.
Animals:	No. We who have teeth are better.

157

Storyteller: Then Crane, who was the leader of the Birds, and Bear, who was the leader of the Animals, had an idea for settling the argument.

Crane: Let's have a ball game. The first side to
            score a goal will win the argument.

Bear: This is a good idea. The side that loses
            will have to accept the penalty given by
            the other side.

Crane: Come, all you Birds. We are going to have a ball game with the Animals to prove we are better.

Bear: Come, all you Animals. We are going to have a ball game with the Birds. We will show them who is better.

Crane: Everyone with wings must come on our side.

Bear: Everyone with teeth must come on our side.

Storyteller: But when the teams were formed, one creature was left out: Bat. He had wings *and* teeth. He flew back and forth between the two sides.

Bat: I have teeth. I must be on the side with you Animals.

Bear: It would not be fair. You have wings. You must be a Bird.

Storyteller: So Bat flew to the other side.

Bat: Take me on your side, for as you see I
                 have wings.

Storyteller:	But the birds laughed at Bat and said . . .
Bird 1:	You are too little to help us.
Bird 2:	We don't want you.
Birds:	Besides, you have teeth. Go away!

166

Storyteller: Then Bat went back to the Animals.

Bat: Please let me join your team. The Birds laughed at me and did not want me.

Animal 1:   You are not very big.

Animal 2:   But sometimes even the small ones can help.

Bear: You may play on our team, but you must hold back and let the bigger Animals play first.

Storyteller:	Two poles were set up as the goalposts at each end of the field, and the game began. Each team played hard because each group wanted to prove it was better than the other. And as they played they argued . . . .
Fox and Deer:	We are swift runners!

Bear: I am strong. I will clear the way for you.

Crane and Hawk: We are even swifter. We will steal the ball before you reach your goal.

170

Bird 1:	See how we can take the ball high into the air.
Bird 2:	You Animals cannot reach us up here.
Animal 1:	It is true that we cannot reach you.
Animal 2:	But we guard our goal well.

Animals:	We will not let you win.
Storyteller:	But the Animals grew tired as the sun began to set, and the Birds began to feel sure they would win.
Crane:	Ha! Ha! I've got the ball!
Storyteller:	Still, the Animals did not give up.
Bear:	I'll stop you!

Storyteller:	But Bear stumbled and fell because it was dark and he could not see.
Animal 1:	Oh, no! Now who will stop Crane?
Storyteller:	Suddenly, a small, dark shape flew onto the field.
Bat:	Now is my chance! I can stop Crane. I will steal the ball from him.

Storyteller:	As Bat darted through the shadows at Crane . . .
Crane:	What?! What was that? Bat has stolen the ball. We must stop Bat, or we will lose the game!
Birds:	Oh, no! We cannot stop Bat! He can see in the dark and we cannot.

Storyteller:	Holding the ball, Bat flew right between the poles at the other end!
Animals:	Hurrah! Hurrah! We've won! We've won!

Bear: Bat, because of you, we won the game. We have proven the Animals are better than the Birds. So you may set the penalty for the Birds.

Storyteller: Bat felt proud. But even though the Birds had laughed at him, he was fair.

Bat: This is your penalty. You Birds must leave this land for half of each year.

Storyteller: So it is that the Birds fly south each winter.

And every day at dusk, Bat still comes flying. He comes to see if the Animals need him to play ball.

The Great Ball Game

Meet the Author

Joseph Bruchac is proud of his Native American heritage. He uses Native American history, animals, and the environment in the stories he writes. Joseph Bruchac is a storyteller too. He tells stories about the mountains where he grew up and tales about Native Americans. Joseph Bruchac wants to share what he knows with his own children and other people too.

Meet the Illustrator

Susan L. Roth has illustrated many children's books. Her favorite art medium is cut-paper collage. This is the medium she used in "The Great Ball Game." Besides writing and illustrating books for children, Susan L. Roth also enjoys art, music, and traveling.

Theme Connections

Within the Selection

Read the questions below, and think about your answers. In small groups, discuss your ideas with one another. Then choose a person to report your group's answers to the class.

- How did the teams choose their players?
- Why was it interesting that Bat won the game?

Across Selections

- In what other story did the characters learn to get along with each other?

Beyond the Selection

- Think about how "The Great Ball Game" is like team games you have played.
- Add items to the Concept/Question Board about games.

Focus Questions What is the best thing about playing on a team with friends? If you are smaller than your teammates, can you still help your team?

The Big Team Relay Race

from ON YOUR MARK, GET SET, GO!
Leonard Kessler
illustrated by Charmie Curran

The animals are playing games. The teams are the Yankees, the Tigers, and the Pirates. Worm wants to play, but she is not on a team.

"All teams line up for the big team relay race," Owl said.

180

Dog, Frog, and Turtle went to the starting line. Duck, Rabbit, and Cat waited down the track. Frog and Turtle each had a little stick.

"Where is my stick?" asked Dog.
"Who has the stick?" asked Owl.
"Get a stick. I need a stick!" yelled Dog.

Worm wiggled over to Owl.

"I am ready, Coach," said Worm.

"Hey, Worm," said Owl. "You can be Dog's stick!"

"Wow! I am on a team!" said Worm. "I'm a Yankee!"

"Okay," said Owl. "Each of you must run with your stick. Then pass it on to your other team member. And remember," said Owl, "the stick must cross the finish line."

"Okay," said little Bird.
"ON YOUR MARK, GET SET, GO!"

Zoom! Down the track they ran.
Cat, Rabbit, and Duck were waiting.
"Here they come," yelled Duck.

Turtle gave his stick to Cat.
Frog gave his stick to Rabbit.
And Dog gave his stick to Duck.

Zoom! Cat, Rabbit, and Duck ran down
the track.

"Duck is winning, Duck is winning!" yelled Dog.
Duck smiled and waved to the cheering crowd.

She tripped over her big web feet and fell into a big mud puddle. Squoosh!

"Get up, Duck," shouted Dog.
"Yikes," yelled Duck,"I am stuck in the mud!"

"Don't worry, Duck," said Worm. "I will win the race for our team."

Worm wiggled and wiggled.

She wiggled past the finish line—first!

"WORM IS THE WINNER!" yelled Spider.

"The Yankees win!" shouted Dog.

"Let's give a cheer for Worm," yelled Owl.
"Squiggle squiggle,
Who can wiggle?
Wiggle wiggle
Wiggle Worm.
Yay, yay, Worm!"

The Big Team Relay Race

Meet the Author

Leonard Kessler was born in Ohio in 1921. He was an artist and designer when he met his wife, who was an author. Together with his wife, Kessler has written and illustrated dozens of children's books. Many of their ideas for books came from their own children. Whenever he can, Kessler enjoys painting with watercolors as a hobby.

Meet the Illustrator

Charmie Curran has always liked to draw. She now lives in Bow, New Hampshire, with her husband Michael, their two children, Allyx and Max, two dogs, two zebra finches, a cat, and eleven assorted chickens.

Theme Connections

Within the Selection

Read the questions below, and think about your answers. In small groups, discuss your ideas with one another. Then choose a person to report your group's answers to the class.

- How was the relay race fair to everyone?
- Why was it surprising that the worm helped win the race?

Across Selections

- How was the relay race different from the other games you have read about?

Beyond the Selection

- Think about relay races. What do you like about them?
- Add items to the Concept/Question Board about games.

Pronunciation Key

a as in **a**t

ā as in l**a**te

â as in c**a**re

ä as in f**a**ther

e as in s**e**t

ē as in m**e**

i as in **i**t

ī as in k**i**te

o as in **o**x

ō as in r**o**se

ô as in b**o**ught and r**a**w

oi as in c**oi**n

o͝o as in b**oo**k

o͞o as in t**oo**

or as in f**or**m

ou as in **ou**t

u as in **u**p

ū as in **u**se

ûr as in t**ur**n; g**er**m, l**ear**n, f**ir**m, w**or**k

ə as in **a**bout, chick**e**n, penc**i**l, cann**o**n, circ**u**s

ch as in **ch**air

hw as in **wh**ich

ng as in ri**ng**

sh as in **sh**op

th as in **th**in

t͟h as in **th**ere

zh as in trea**s**ure

The mark (′) is placed after a syllable with a heavy accent, as in **chicken** (chik′ ən).
The mark (′)after a syllable shows a lighter accent, as in **disappear** (dis′ ə pēr′).

196

Glossary

A

argument (är′ gyə mənt) *n.* A disagreement or debate.

awful (ŏ fəl) *adj.* Bad or unpleasant.

awhile (ə hwīl′) *adv.* For a length of time.

B

brave (brāv) *adj.* To show courage; to not be afraid.

business (biz′ nis) *n.* Job; work.

button (but′ ən) *n.* A small disk to fasten clothing.

C

crabby (krab′ ē) *adj.* Grumpy.

crash (krash) *v.* To fall and hit the ground hard.

creature (krē′ chər) *n.* A living person or animal.

cross (krôs) *adj.* Angry. *v.* To go over.

customer (kus′ tə mər) *n.* A person who buys something.

D

dandelion (dan′ də lī′ ən) *n.* A plant that has a bright yellow flower.

dash (dash) *v.* To run quickly.

dew (do͞o) *n.* Water droplets that form on grass and go away as the air cools.

E

enormous (i nor′ məs) *adj.* Very big.

F

flick (flik) *v.* To touch or hit with a quick, light push.

197

Pronunciation Key: at; lāte; câre; fäther; set; mē; **i**t; kīte; **o**x; rōse; ô in b**ou**ght; c**oi**n; b**oo**k; t**oo**; f**or**m; **ou**t; **u**p; ūse; tûrn; ə sound in **a**bout, chick**e**n, penc**i**l, cann**o**n, circ**u**s; **ch**air; hw in **wh**ich; ri**ng**; **sh**op; **th**in; **th**ere; zh in trea**s**ure.

flop (flop) *v.* To fall suddenly.

fourth (fôrth) *adj.* Number four in order.

frightened (frīt′ ənd) *adj.* Afraid; scared.

G

giggle (gig′ əl) *n.* A short laugh. *v.* To laugh with a short laugh.

gnarled (närld) *adj.* Twisted; lumpy.

goalposts (gōl′ pōsts) *n.* A pair of posts connected by a crossbar that forms a goal in a game such as football.

grouchy (grou′ chē) *adj.* In a bad mood.

ground (ground) *n.* The earth; dirt.

grumble (grum′ bəl) *v.* To rumble.

H

hare (hâr) *n.* A gray or brown animal that looks like a rabbit, but is larger and has long ears.

hare

J

joke (jōk) *n.* Something that won't ever work; something that is not serious.

junk (jungk) *n.* Something that is not worth anything; trash.

L

laugh (laf) *v.* To make a sound that shows something is funny.

laughter (laf′ tər) *n.* The sound a person makes when something is funny.

laze (lāz) *v.* To relax; to rest.

M

meadow (med′ ō) *n.* An open field covered with grasses and sometimes wildflowers.

meadow

N

noise (noiz) *n.* A loud sound.

nuzzle (nuz′ əl) *v.* To gently rub with the nose or snout.

P

pace (pās) *n.* The speed of walking or running.

paw (pô) *n.* The foot of an animal; usually with claws.

penalty (pen′ əl tē) *n.* A punishment.

perhaps (pər haps′) *adv.* Maybe.

picky (pik′ ē) *adj.* Hard to please.

plod (plod) *v.* To walk slowly and heavily.

plop (plop) *v.* To drop or fall with a heavy landing.

prove (pro͞ov) *v.* To show that something is true.

purr (pûr) *v.* A sound a cat makes when it is happy.

Q

quite (kwīt) *adv.* Very.

R

relay race (rē′ lā rās) *n.* A team race in which each team member takes a turn and completes only one part of the race.

reply (ri plī′) *v.* To answer; to say.

rescue (res′ kū) *v.* To save from danger.

ripe (rīp) *adj.* Fully grown; ready for eating.

S

shade (shād) *v.* To give cover from the sun.

shout (shout) *v.* To call loudly; to yell.

smack (smak) *v.* To hit or clap.

sour (sou′ ər) *adj.* Having a tart taste, like lemon juice.

spider (spī′ dər) *n.* A small eight-legged animal that spins and lives in a web.

stomp (stomp) *v.* To stamp with the foot.

stumble (stum′ bəl) *v.* To trip.

swift (swift) *adj.* Quick.

T

thirsty (thûr′ stē) *adj.* Needing a drink.

thud (thud) *n.* The sound made when something or someone falls.

tired (tīrd) *adj.* Sleepy.

tortoise (tor′ təs) *n.* A large land turtle.

tortoise

tower (tou′ r) *v.* To be much
taller than.

trip (trip) *v.* To hit a foot
against something so as
to fall.

tumble (tum′ bəl) *v.* To fall
down.

V

vine (vīn) *n.* A plant that has
a very long stem. A vine can
grow along the ground or up
a wall.

vine

W

wiggle (wig′ əl) *v.* To squirm
or twist.